Steven K. Browning
212 College St
DeQuincy, LA. 70633
337-263-0417
Steven@middlemanconsulting.com

And then I came home to you

When Love Refuses to Die

by

Steven K. Browning

Introduction

I met her by chance. I had resided in the area a year or so ago, but I had not met many people there. When I met Kristy, I knew that I had not yet lived before. I had been there before, made friends there, worked there and functioned as part of society there but I never lived there before. I started living there when I first met Kristy. She was beautiful, tiny, and flawless as far as I could tell. I thought to myself, she must have a terrible personality, no one is that perfect and a great person, right?

The first time I spoke to her, I do not even know what we talked about. We were making small talk and trying to seem cool to each other, like young people do and I thought I was doing a rather good job.

I had successfully made her laugh a few times and that seemed like a win. The longer we spoke, the more I debunked my theory that she must be a terrible person. She was intelligent, well-spoken, and as positive as you could expect a teenager to be.

I was also a teenager, but I had been "out of the house" for a while and normally I did not get along with other teens.

I always seemed to fit better with the older crowds. When I spoke to Kristy, the conversation just seemed to flow. I was doubtful when I met her, but my doubt turned out to be misplaced. This girl was interesting and beautiful.

This book is about a real connection between two soul mates. In this book, you will find romance, love, attraction, and even good old boring data. I am writing this book in secret, no one knows that I am writing this book. Especially not Kristy. She will not find out until it is published, and she will have to buy it to find out what is inside of it!

After all these years, I still find her interesting and I am looking forward to watching her open the book for the first time.

What is love? Some describe it as a feeling that washes over you when you meet the right person and I believe that but let us not forget that love is also an action that we can take. As humans, we can love.

Why am I writing this? Because too many times I have heard people say, "I just do not love her or him anymore". My response is, then love them. What are you waiting for?

You cannot sit around and wait for love to happen. That loving feeling that washes over you is meant to initiate a connection, not last forever and be the only thing you have.

If you are married or dating and start doubting whether you love your partner then ask yourself, "am I loving them?". What I mean is, when you met the person and fell head over heels, you were doing everything in the world that you could for them. You were loving them. If you did that now, would you still feel the same?

If you were doing everything to ensure someone's happiness, would you care if you did a little more than them? Likely not. Why? Because you would be loving them instead of measuring who was doing what.

Remember when they were willing to do anything for you? They were loving you and they also did not care who was putting in what effort. It is a good possibility that they would follow your lead and start loving you back, if you put in the effort.

I am not saying that there are not bad relationships, but wouldn't you want to know for sure before you gave up? In this book, I will tell the story from one of my first loves and my last love. In my case, they happen to be the same person.

Chapter 1 – What is Love

What exactly is love? It is defined as an intense feeling of deep affection and while that is not wrong, it does leave room for elaboration. Love is something that dominates your entire being. You can fight love and throw facts and logic at it all day long, but it does not care. It just keeps taking you over twenty-four hours a day until the fight in you is gone.

Love does not live by society's rules, it takes who it wants, when it wants and does what it wants. When we do manage to fight love, it leaves us with doubt, sadness, and a feeling of emptiness.

If we fight love long enough, we may be left with a thick leather exterior on our hearts that allows us to not feel pain but also does not allow us to feel joy or happiness.

Why would we fight love? One reason is because we live by the rules of society. If a person is spoken for, we do not want to break up their relationship, so we fight our love of that person.

Other times, we are afraid of opening ourselves up and being exposed to pain. We worry that if the relationship does not work out, we will have to feel the heartbreak and we fear that so much we refuse to take the chance.

Sometimes we confuse lust and desire with love, it is easy to do and when we do this, it often results in broken friendships, anger, and pain.

Real love however cannot be denied, and it lasts a lifetime. Real love lasts even if you swear each other off forever and move far away from each other. Even if you pledge yourself to another person, you cannot eliminate real love, you can only lock it away where it will slowly eat at you forever. I can attest to this personally and I will show you why as we travel through my own story together.

How do you know when love is real? Does it come with a guarantee? Does it have identifying markings? No, but if you pay attention to your inner self, you just may be able to tell when you are in love.

I remember the first time I saw Kristy; she was at her mom's mailbox in Red Oak, Tx. I was staying with some friends that happened to be her neighbor's while I was in between construction jobs.

She was young, already married and had a young child. She was also beautiful, sweet and had a great personality. I never did pinpoint what it was about her that caught me off guard, maybe because I thought everything about her was perfect.

When I saw her, I believed in love at first sight. In hindsight, I think I saw that we were meant to be together. Sadly, you can be meant for each other and still not end up together, unfortunately, this is a common occurrence.

In the case of Kristy and I, we both fought love and tried not to love each other but as I said before, real love will not be denied.

Now, before you paint me as a home wrecker, know that I kept my distance and I was nothing more than a friend… for a while. I felt what I felt, but I did not dare say it out loud. And besides that, I had little to do with the downfall of her relationship except for being too close and being her soul mate. I was willing to keep my feelings to myself forever.

No, I just kept on doing my thing, being young, hanging out with friends and doing my best to ignore the way I felt about her. I had all intentions of getting over it and going about my business. I never thought I would have a chance because she was taken but I was wrong.

I should have known something was going to happen because I could tell that she was feeling the same way as I did. I was not sure why she felt the same way. Was the feeling real love for her as well or was it only lust?

After all, I was young, maybe eighteen or nineteen, blond headed, six feet three inches tall and in great shape. I had been working as an ironworker for the past year, so I had some grit and I had a sense of humor that kept people laughing. Seeing others laugh has always been important to me. Whatever I lacked in handsomeness, I made up for in humor.

For now, let us discuss the power of love over young people. I fell in love a few times when I was young, and it seemed like I was powerless to prevent it. It seemed like certain types of girls had an something unexplainable that I could not resist.

As I grew into my late teens, I was better at controlling these feelings and only allowed them to form if the girl felt the same way. Afterall, who wants to be in love with someone that does not feel the same way?

Even though I had grown into a person with a little self-control, I still managed to fall for Kristy. This time was different though, it was stronger and more meaningful.

Still I resisted. I suffered quietly because my heart wanted her to know how I felt. I wanted her to know how I felt, I wanted everyone to know how I felt but I kept it to myself.

Well I did not say the words anyway, I am certain that my friends could tell how I felt and maybe she could too. That is for her to say, not me.

I am a person that believes in doing the right thing, even when it is hard but when I was eighteen years old, my willpower was less than strong. That is an excuse but that does not mean it is wrong.

What dictates the line between right and wrong, anyway? I realize it is wrong to yearn for a person that is married to someone else but what about letting your soul mate get away without even speaking up, is that wrong?

Is it ok to be unfulfilled for a lifetime because you showed up too late? Is it fair to her to let her get away knowing that she will think about you forever and you about her?

I am not trying to justify anything; I only ask you to keep an open mind and think it through before siding with society's rules.

What if she had been part of an arranged marriage and fell in love with someone else? Would it be acceptable that she wanted someone else? In this case, she was married to the wrong person and everyone silently knew it.

Before I met Kristy, I did not believe in soulmates, in fact, I thought that marriage was tied to effort. If both parties worked hard at being happily married, it would be so. If one of them did not want to work at it, it would not last. That was my way of thinking.

Now, I still somewhat believe this, but I also believe in true love. I even believe that there just may only be one true love for each of us. If that one true love is never found, then you may wind up in a marriage that you hate coming home to. How terrible would that be?

I also believe that you must work at anything to make it successful. You can be married to your soulmate and still let it fail. We will talk more about love in the form of a verb later in the book.

Most people recommend marriage counselling to the couples that are unhappy, and I do not disagree, but I also recommend facing facts. If you hate each other, you may not be right for each other.

If that is the case, why would you stay together? For the sake of your kids? Because it is comfortable? Maybe you do not want to split up the bills or cannot pay them alone?

None of these are important enough to stay unhappily married for your entire one and only life. And if your kids are watching you suffer forever, that is a terrible lesson to teach them. You cannot find your true love if you are busy being home with someone that you wish you were not with.

See the marriage counsellor but only long enough to make sure you should or should not be together. If it turns out to be a should not, get out immediately.

Chapter 2 – The first Kiss

A million times I told myself I was just young and weak, and I needed to strengthen myself. Maybe so, and I did manage to contain myself for a while but when her relationship took a dive, it was too much for me.

I was drawn to her and she was drawn to me, I was still resisting but I was losing the battle. After a few friendly weeks of "harmless" flirting, we ended up having a moment and I knew that I was changed forever. I was addicted to her and like any person with an addiction, I would do almost anything to get my fix.

I knew that I was in love with this girl and I knew that others would be hurt because of it but the love for her overpowered my need to do the so-called "right thing".

Our moment was a simple kiss, but it was so much more than that. We had somehow touched our lips together and welded our hearts together at the same time.

We were visiting one afternoon, and we kept talking and making jokes about silly things but at the same time, we kept moving closer to each other. My heart was beating fast and I wanted to either kiss her and see if it killed me or make an excuse and leave so I could gather my strength and come back brave.

My words were like a panic in my head but somehow, they were smooth and calm when they left my mouth. Who the hell was that talking? Was that my voice because it certainly did not match my thoughts.

At some point, I accepted that it was my voice and I was able to calm down a little. Enough that I did not have a heart attack or run out of the room.

We eventually got close enough to touch each other, not sexually, just casually. Like a bumping of the knees but we did not pull them back apart. We stayed touching each other. After a short while, I moved like I was uncomfortable and need to adjust my posture, but I could not feel anything except the pounding of my heart.

My skin was tingling, my head was floating, and my heart seemed to be beating to a rhythm. I readjusted so I could get even closer to her and when I did, she did the same. We were touching and I looked at her again and tried to find something that I did not like. I wanted an anchor point that I could use that would bring me back to reality, but I did not find one.

I looked her up and down from her pretty little face down to her toes and there was nothing that I did not like. Hell, there was nothing that I did not love about her.

Just as I thought I was going to die, our eyes locked and our lips touched, and I found a way to love her even more. We kissed for a long time and then pulled back and smiled at each other.

The ice had been broken but I was still feeling like I might explode. We stayed together for several hours and some things happened, but they are hard to remember. I just remember holding her in my arms and kissing her and wondering how I got this lucky.

Chapter 3 – Our Very Own Version of Dating

When we had first met, I was electrified by her presence and this never changed. When I was with her, I was completely tuned into her. There was no one else or anything else in the room. My focus was on Kristy.

I was young and dumb, but I was smart enough to know this girl had my heart at her disposal. She could crush me at any moment and instead of being afraid of it, I embraced it. If she crushed my heart, I would just have to die but in no way did I want to take my heart away from her.

We were just two kids in love, and we did not have a ton of money, so our dates were nothing extravagant. In fact, if we would have been wealthy, we would not have known what to do with the money.

We probably would have upsized our meals at Taco Bueno and McDonalds! That is pretty much the level we were playing on. We were just two broke kids starting out in the world and finding our way but now, we were finding our way together.

I have been asked before if I know why I never got strung out on any drugs when I was a teenager and one answer is that I could not afford them. I had things I wanted and needed, and I needed to be able to pay for them. One of those things was the love of my life whom I had just kissed for the first time.

We had many cheap dates, but we were happy to just sit and talk for hours or watch television together. It was great, I am not sure what we watched or where we went on dates, but I can remember that it was great, and my heart was full.

There were times when we walked around downtown Dallas and often, we managed to buy beer and wine coolers and just sit around and laugh together at home.

When I think about these simple times and how happy we were it makes me smile. How could we be so happy even though we had nothing and had no idea what we were planning for in the future? We only knew that we were together and that made us happy.

We did not need plans; we would face whatever came at us and fight our way through it. That is the beautiful thing about being young. Of course, later in life, we learned to prepare for the future, after all, we had families to think of.

When lovers first meet, it a natural desire to spend as much time together as possible. It does not matter if you are doing something fun like shopping or going to an amusement park or something boring, like folding socks. You just want to be together.

It was no different for us, we wanted to be together. If we were doing boring things, we wanted to do them together and we certainly did not plan to do fun things separately. We planned everything together.

I had friends that would plan entire weekends apart from their spouses and I could not imagine it. I know we were a new couple, but I could not imagine spending a weekend without Kristy.

To zip ahead to the future for a moment, I still cannot imagine spending a weekend without Kristy. That is just not how we do things. We are always better off together and we intend to stay that way.

I know others that plan time away from each other and that seems to work for them, but I do not have anyone that I would rather hang around than my darling wife.

Chapter 4 – Being Young

We had a long run of pure happiness and I thought it would never end but as it turns out, troubled times were ahead.

We were not spending time apart, but we were also young and susceptible to the dangers of bad environments. We still wanted to fit into the world instead of carving out our own path.

Over time, we had grown fond of drinking and hosting cook outs as well as hanging out with many people. We went to bars and clubs and all kind of different events. We were young and impressionable, and this is what all the older couples did so we thought we had to do the same.

As we went to the bars and met new people, our circle grew. It seemed like we knew someone everywhere we went.

While this was a good thing most of the time. There are a few bad people around, no matter where you go. We were getting hit on by strangers and sometimes friends and when this happens long enough to a young couple, it leaves room for mistakes.

I will not go into details here, but I was the first one to make one of these mistakes and this led to other mistakes by both of us.

I never thought bad of her, but I hated the things we had done to each other. I had opened this door and I could not close it. I tried to close it a few times but, in the end, I just walked away.

I just could not get past all we had been through. She gave me a chance to hit the reset button once and I tried but I just could not do it. In short, I missed our second chance because I was protecting my ego and pride. If I had been a little more mature, I would have taken that chance and we would not have missed over twenty years of each other's lives, but I must look on the bright side. I have a wonderful son that may not have happened if we had not walked away.

Chapter 5 – Torn Apart

For a long time, if I stopped long enough, I was overwhelmed by doubt, disappointment, and disbelief that things could go so wrong. It seemed like the woman I had cared so much for now hated me.

How did I let this happen? I still loved her and wanted her by me every second of the day, but I could not do anything about it. This was one of those times when I learned that you must appreciate what you have before it is gone.

We tried to make it work once more before we walked away for good, but the attempt was feeble. I cannot speak for her, but my heart was not in it. I felt as though we were putting off the inevitable.

I wanted to be the man she needed but my confidence level was too low at the time. In the end, there was just too much water under the bridge, and we split up again.

When we split up this time, it was over and we both knew it. She stayed in Dallas and I went off to my hometown in Louisiana.

I went to work in the refineries again and got busy building the financial part of my life. I thought that she might call and say that she wanted to try again but she never did.

So many times, when I had accomplished something, I wanted to be able to share that moment with her. To tell her about it and share the moment but it was not in the cards.

I was heartbroken and wanted to talk to her and the kids and her younger brothers that I felt were my family, but I did not call. I was afraid that she would answer and if she did, I would say things to get us back together.

I know she wanted the same, but we would only end up putting ourselves through hell again. I decided that I had to just go through the pain and get over it. We had already hurt each other so much and I could not allow us to do it again.

Chapter 6 – Starting Over

Eventually, I did get over the pain and I started to live and build a life again. I was still young, and I made new friends that were also young, and we started to hang out. I started to rebuild my broken-down self into something stronger than I was before. I was a better person than I had been before, but I was still not over Kristy. I began to wonder if I would ever stop thinking about her.

Now, I know that the answer is no. I will never stop thinking about her even though she is back in my life.

My friends would take me out to clubs, and we would all drink and make fun of each other and other people and it was a great time until it started to get late.

It never failed; my friends were always trying to get me to "hook up" with someone at one of these bars. They would drag some pretty girl in front of me and introduce us, but I was not ready for this.

I wanted to do my friends right so I would talk to the girl for a while but then I would just walk away and not come back. Several times, I left the club without saying goodbye to my friends at all after one of these attempts to "hook me up".

They thought I was just shy and needed help getting over the hump, but the truth is, I was not over Kristy and every pretty girl I spoke to felt like I was killing my memories of her.

It felt like her memories were all I had left of her and I was not ready for someone to come along and erase them. I did not realize it at the time, but those memories were permanent and could not be erased. I also did not know that they were permanent for Kristy as well.

Eventually, I got past this and went about my life. I got married, had a child, and worked hard at life but that marriage did not last. I got divorced and spent a short time away from my son but eventually he came to live with me, and I raised him the best way I knew how. I had help along the way, a lot of help and it was appreciated and necessary. Also, his mother was still in his life, but she was doing her thing and my son, and I were together for a lot of years before I had a stable relationship.

After my divorce, I dated for a while. I even dated seriously a few times, but nothing ever worked out. There was always something that seemed to easily tear those relationships apart.

After feeling like an idiot a few times, I decided that I would keep doing the dating thing and see if I could find something that would last but I never did. At some point, I decided that there would only be one rocking chair on my porch when I got older, but it would be a nice porch.

While I was doing my thing and playing the game of life, I was also climbing the corporate ladder and building a better future for myself and my son.

That was my main goal and I did well at it. At some point, I decided that being happily married was not in the cards for me, so I decided that being successful in my career was the next best thing.

I worked on myself and headed in the right direction and did great. I obtained and left jobs that most people only dream of. I helped others achieve their goals and this helped me grow even more.

I learned, helped others learn and never looked back. When I poured myself into my career, I lost part of myself but that was okay because I found something else. I found the ability to be the best at whatever I wanted to do. I was focused on climbing the ladder and finding success in my every move.

I still went to all my son's events and attended everything I should have, and I have those great memories, but I found it increasingly difficult to disconnect from my work.

I loved my work and I needed it and it was obvious that I was absorbed in it. Other people looked at me like I was crazy, like I was obsessed and maybe I was but at the time, it hurt no one so I did not mind being obsessed.

When I reached a certain rung on the ladder, I noticed that my career was not filling the emptiness inside of me. I worked harder and climber higher to fill the hole, but I just could not make the feeling go away.

I tried other things, I focused on my health and got in great shape and I learned to play the game of life even better, but nothing could suppress the feeling of being incomplete.

I started new hobbies, but I rarely made time for them. I changed the types of places that I drank at along with the people that I drank with and that seemed to help a little, but I really was not much of a drinker.

I was great at being around people when it came to work but when I was on personal time, I wanted to be away from the crowds. This is great unless you are alone then it feels like you are obligated to be out and about. I used to think I was pitiful when I stayed home by myself but that was just ego and worrying about what others think.

I find that ego is something we should check often. If left unchecked, it can get out of control. An uncontrolled ego can be our destruction.

I am not talking about ego as in cockiness, I am talking about ego as in wounded pride. If we allow our ego to control us, we are always subject to the emotions that follow.

We do things that we do not want to do, and we say things that we would never say because of our egos. There were many times that my ego affected my life and I can probably recall each one, if I were to spend enough time thinking about it.

In time, I learned to recognize my ego and control it. No longer does ego in any form control my life. When I do have a moment. I recognize it and make sure that I am doing everything I can to correct the situation.

Chapter 7 – Accepting the Facts

I was riding home from work one afternoon and thinking about how to fill the emptiness in my life and what I wanted to do next, and I thought about someone from my past.

Over twenty years ago from my past to be more specific. A thought of Kristy came to me out of the blue and I wondered how she was and what she had done with her life.

When I had this thought, social media was already a thing so I decided to look her up and see what I could find. I found her after making friends with about twenty women that had the same name and lived in her area.

I found out that she was married, and I managed to see a picture of her with her family and it made me smile. That was the only thing I did was glance at her profile and then I was simply happy that she was happy. Kristy was always very family oriented and I was happy to see her surrounded by family.

I did not make any moves to contact her because she was a married woman. I went on with my life and did not look her up again, but I still had lingering thoughts about her and the times we had together so many years ago.

I wondered how I ever let her get away. Was it worth it to move on with my life back then? As humans, we tend to second guess our decisions, especially when the decisions were made over twenty years ago.

I tried to stop thinking about her after that, and for the most part, I was successful but occasionally, I found my thoughts on her and the old days when we were together.

I mean, I did not think about her constantly, but I did think back often to those days and how happy we were together. I could even remember her smile and how pretty she was. Not just exterior beauty, she had a personality that was every bit as beautiful as she was.

I compared my life to those moments from so many years before and decided that I had never loved any woman as much as her. I had not thought about it in years, but I again wondered if there really is such a thing as soul mates.

If there really are soul mates in this world, is it possible to keep them apart for a lifetime? After thinking for a while, I determine that soul mates are a myth and that I am just hung up on my past and need to get over it.

I mean, would the universe allow two beings that were meant for each other to suffer a lifetime of being apart? No way! And if we were soul mates, would I allow us to be apart just because it is considered the right thing to do by other flawed members of society?

These are deep questions that do not have an easy answer. I decide that the best thing to do is stop thinking about it and refocus on my career.

I pick up the phone to call our sales team and set up a meeting to go over the pipeline and forecasting for our region and this helps me forget about her for a while.

I had been sinking into my thoughts for several minutes and I was afraid of what I might find down there if I had sunk too low. I reach each member of my sales team and have them meet me to go over the numbers and then I sit my phone down and it rings.

I pick up the phone and I notice it is just a number with no contact and I rarely answer these. These calls are usually about my car's extended warranty and I just do not answer them. If they leave a message and it is legitimate, I call them back.

I do notice that this number comes from Grand Prairie, Texas and that intrigues me. Grand Prairie was close to where Kristy and I spent our time together. For a moment, I wonder if the universe is trying to tell me something and then I dismiss it.

I place my phone back on the console of my seat and keep driving. I totally dismiss the thought of Grand Prairie and Kristy and I start mentally preparing for the sales meeting. I have many questions about our forecast, and I am excited to hear from the team.

When I arrived at home, I go through my daily routine and interact with my son as much as I can. He is a full-blown teenager at this time, and we can only interact so much peacefully. We love each other but, we do not spend much time together unless it is during an outing or event.

As I am laying down to go to sleep for the night, I allow my thoughts to drift and do what they want to do, and they return to thinking about her. I wonder if she has ever thought about me over the years. I wonder if she even remembers me and then I think well yes of course she remembers me! Just kidding but my guess is that she remembers me because our time together meant so much to me.

It has been almost twenty-three years since we last saw each other, I wonder if she even remembers what I look like. The last time we saw each other, she was throwing my stuff over the balcony handrail at her apartment, that must leave a memory, right?

After realizing that I must be some sort of weird person for thinking about her from so long ago, I drift off, but I am excited about my upcoming meeting and the day ahead.

Chapter 8 - The Call That Changed It All

I arrived at my office early the next morning. I rearranged my office to accommodate the group, printed out a few documents for everyone and proofread my presentation again. I was ready to get this meeting started and hear some exciting news.

I followed up with the team and confirmed that everyone was coming and then I took it a step farther, I called some of the clients that I often dealt with directly and got some fresh market data from them. I was technically not a salesperson but if you know me then you know that everyone is a salesperson in my mind.

If you are in management and I hear you say that you cannot sell, I will be forced to have a conversation with you and ask many questions until one of us changes our minds. In many ways, management is sales.

I wanted to have something to contribute to the meeting and show the team that I was engaged and knew what it was like to sell to our customers. That is how important this meeting was to me. I wanted everything to be perfect.

You are probably asking yourself why I am writing all of this about a meeting when I am trying to tell a love story and I do not blame you but hang in there, the reason will become clear shortly.

I am in anticipation of this meeting all day long. The meeting is at two pm and it seems to take forever to make it to lunch. I stayed busy but I really struggle to stay focused on the work I am doing. For lunch, I meet with some clients but as soon as it is over, I rush back to my office to check one last time and make sure I am ready.

At around one pm, the team starts arriving and I make coffee and espresso for everyone that is interested. Everyone knows I am careful in selecting my coffee and I make an awesome espresso, so they are popular with the team. Maybe it is not that my coffee is awesome, maybe they just do not know the difference.

When the entire team is settled, we begin our meeting. I start out with setting the expectations that I have for everyone and then I ask the same from them. Once we make it through expectations, we begin a round table discussion of each representative's region and what they are planning on bringing to the table.

During this time, it is my job to dig for conflict by asking questions and guiding the conversation to the tough places where no one wants to go. I enjoy this because I learn from it every time I do it. When you get past the mask that we all wear, the person we want everyone to think we are and find the real person inside, you always learn something.

We are almost halfway through the round table discussion and my phone vibrates. I look at it and it is the same number from Grand Prairie, Tx so I flip it over and ignore it. It would have to be especially important for me to answer during this meeting.

A few seconds later, I receive a text from the same number. The text stated, "hey old friend, give me a call when you get time". I responded, "my apologies, I am only getting a number without a name, who is this?" Here it comes, wait for it.

The response I got was only one word, but it changed everything. The response simply said, "Kristy". I could not have been more surprised if it would have been a call from Snoop Dogg.

When I read this response, my heart skipped a beat. I stared at it for a moment in disbelief and then I excused myself from the meeting. Did I get busted when I was thinking about her? Was she able to see that I had looked her up on Facebook? How could she know that I was thinking about her?

A million thoughts ran through my mind and an excitement ran through me. I was like a little kid that just received a gift that I had been wanting for a long time.

I called and heard a voice that I had not heard in twenty-three years and I was so happy to hear it. I expected to feel awkward when we spoke, but it was like we had seen each other yesterday.

We started talking like we were supposed to be talking to each other. I'm not one to believe in destiny or that God has your plan laid out for you. I believe we are all self-made. We are a product of our choices. Knowing this, you can imagine how odd these thoughts were to me. There had to be some logical explanation, right?

If you believe having a soulmate is logical, then yes. If you are skeptical about that then call it coincidence if you like.

There was no awkwardness and the conversation just flowed. I learned that she was in process of a divorce and had been thinking about me for some time now. I told her that I had thought of her out of the blue and we had to wonder if it was just a coincidence or something more. We talked like we had never been apart. While it seemed odd that we would do this, it felt perfectly natural.

I revisited this many times because it seems like more that coincidence. Imagine two people that have not seen each other in twenty-three years and had no reason to think about each other. These two people start to think of each other at the same time out of the blue. What are the odds?

Could it be that we are truly connected and when she thought about me, I could feel it? I will leave that up to you to decide. I will not try to sway your opinion, but I will say that I believe it was more than chance.

Even after years have passed, I still believe it was more than coincidence. I'm not saying it was a miracle but maybe an intervention.

After what seemed like a few minutes, I looked at my watch and I had been on the phone for over an hour. I got off the phone and walked back to my office to find my meeting over and everything I had asked for completed and waiting on me. What a great team, right?

I called the members of my team and explained what had just happened and they were all excited for me and excused me for leaving the meeting and not returning. I say again, what a great team, right?

I called Kristy again later that afternoon and we talked for hours and before it was over, I was making plans to drive to Dallas for the upcoming weekend.

If you stop and think about that is kind of crazy, but I think love is crazy. One minute I am thinking about a girl that I have not seen in twenty-three years with no intention of ever seeing her again and the next thing I know; I am making plans to drive six hours to visit her.

We had no idea what to expect. From my point of view, I did not know what I was getting into. I had not spoken to her in years, she could be a complete psycho for all I knew.

I tried to see myself from her point of view and asked myself what she must be thinking. Why would this guy just pack up and drive six hours to meet her out of the blue? Is there something wrong with him? Can he not find a girl in his own town? If she ever actually thought these things, she never said them to me, but I am the type that overthinks everything, so it crossed my mind.

Yes. this trip was sudden, and it invited some self-doubt but that was brief. I knew in my heart that this trip was the right thing to do. If I had not taken this trip, I have no idea where I would be today, but I know it could not top where I am right now.

Chapter 9 – Kristy Trip

I went to the office early that Friday morning and made sure everything was in order before I left and headed to Dallas. I was excited and a little nervous which is a little hard for me to admit. As I said before, nervous is not my thing and it feels very awkward to me. I feel bad for people that allow themselves to be naturally nervous.

Once I got on the road, I called Kristy and talked to her for quite a while and then I hit an area where the cell phone signal was in and out so I just rode for a while.

As I rode in silence, I wondered what it would be like to see her after all these years. To wrap my arms around her and hug her. I thought back to the days when we were young and together and remembered how it felt to hug her. She had a way of defying physics and being able to squeeze tighter that you would expect from a ninety-pound woman. Again, I felt a little nervous but mostly because I was super excited.

I want to emphasize that I do not get nervous often. In fact, people have joked about the world ending and me standing there calmly watching it while everyone else is panicking. Again, nervous is just not my thing.

I wondered how this tiny little woman could make me nervous and then it occurred to me that she was not doing this to me. I was doing it to myself. I had to find a way to relax. The last thing I wanted to do was be a nervous wreck when I saw her for the first time in so many years.

Relaxing is not my thing either. I like to be busy and I live for productivity, no matter what we are doing, I want it to be efficient and productive. In this case, I had to slow myself down and relax.

I drove for about six hours and then arrived at the Hotel just as it was getting dark. We were planning to check in and then go out to dinner and just enjoy some conversation and catch up.

If you are thinking that this encounter was about sex, you are wrong. I mean, we are two grown adults that can do whatever we want, but this meeting was about so much more than that.

We met in the parking lot and hugged for a long time. She struggled to look me in the eye for more than a second or two and I could see why. It had been so long since we had seen each other, she was not sure if I was who she remembered.

After all, I was dressed for work and I was close to double the age I was when we last saw each other. Later in the book, I will talk more about how people change and grow and you will see that I was not the boy she knew so many years ago but for now, let us focus on this encounter.

After we got on the elevator and started talking, she started to loosen up and I did too. We picked up dinner and had some drinks and talked all night. It was a great time and we were already making plans to see each other again before the weekend was even over.

It was like we had never been apart. I mean, we had a huge piece of our lives that took place without each other, but it was almost like that was something we had to go through to get to here.

Do not get me wrong, there are many things that neither of us would ever change, we love our kids and friends and family that we built during this time apart, but it is possible that we were never complete without each other.

We spent two amazing days and nights together. We laughed so hard that our faces were sore, and I felt like I had it all. I was as happy as I could ever remember being and I could not get over the fact that we had been apart for so long and not only remembered each other but still loved each other.

Of course, we both knew that we wanted more than two days together, we wanted to stay together and never be apart again. Instead, we went back to our lives and started preparing to see each other as often as possible.

When I was leaving to head home, we had our sad moment, but we decided then and there that we would be together, forever. We made a commitment to each other and went off to prepare our lives so that we could be together.

Many of you may be thinking that we jumped into this thing and there is no way that what we were feeling after all these years is love. You may also think that we were just feeling lust for each other and that we were caught up in the moment, but I can tell you that this was different.

From the moment she sent the text with her name, I knew exactly where this was going and where we would end up. I had to have her, and I intended to have her. I had a second chance and I was not about to let her get away again. This time, I would break her ankle so she would not be able to run, I am kidding. I thought I would add a little humor just to break up the monotony.

From the moment I heard her voice, I was in love with her all over again. Believe what you want but this was more than two compatible people falling for each other, this was two soulmates catching up.

If you ask my friends, they will tell you that I was incapable of loving someone this way and this much. They will tell you that I was very methodical, and I was not superstitious and that I believe there is a logical explanation for everything.

They will also tell you that I was never one to discuss love much less write a book about the woman I love. Many who know me or who knew me over the years will be in disbelief when they see this book.

Chapter 10 – Closing Out the Past

When I got back from Dallas, I had several things to clean up. First, I had to bring my son up to speed on what was going on. He did not know that our lives were about to change, and he needed to be ready.

At some point, he would meet Kristy and I did not want it to be a shock. He was a teenager and hard enough to deal with as it was, so I wanted to take my best shot at this.

I sat him down and told him everything that was about to happen, and he took about two seconds to act like he understood and then went on his way. I could see trouble in the future, but I did not see a way to stop it. In hindsight, it would have been better to go ahead and make him angry then than to let him get away without understanding what was about to happen.

I left that to simmer and assumed I had more time and I would discuss it with him again later.

Next, I had to end a few things that had been going on before Kristy had called me and I wanted to end them quickly. I made it through that process and then turned my focus to the other big changes I had to make.

I had to change my work habits. My work habits were great for work, but they allowed no room for a relationship especially one that was six hours away.

I planned with my direct manager and worked with my team to inspire autonomy and encouraged them to delegate and challenge the people that reported to them. This helped everyone focus on the things that would grow them into stronger leaders and would also free up a little of my time and allow me to have time for a love life.

Chapter 11 – A Turning Point

I started travelling every weekend to Dallas and spending time with Kristy. My son came with me a couple of times but most of the time, he avoided the trips.

I found myself with a lot of driving time and most of that was spent on the phone but some of it allowed me to think and process what was going on in my life. This time was valuable.

After a while, I started leaving work earlier on Fridays to travel and get a head start on my way to Dallas. Fortunately, I had an excellent team that could cover our region and call me when they needed me. I was on the road a lot and I learned a lot about skype meetings and go to meetings.

We found many places to stay that were so much better than a hotel. We stayed in log cabins that were amazing, we stayed in a remodelled airstream trailer and all kinds of different places. It was a lot of fun and we made a lot of memories.

We rented a big house for a weekend and invited many family members for a weekend so we could catch up and learn about each other. We had some great times with some great people.

I had not seen these people in over twenty years and they still treated me like family. They still treat me like family today and I am thankful to have them.

After a few months of travelling all the time, I was getting tired and it was beginning to show in my performance as well as my ability to drive and stay awake for long periods.

I found myself fighting sleep every time I sat down and especially when I got behind the wheel. I knew something had to change. A man can only sing and ride with the windows down for so long before he gets sleepy again.

When Kristy and I met again, we talked about the future and where we were headed, and we decided to begin planning for her to move to my hometown with me.

This would be a huge change for her, and I am proud of her for taking this leap with me. She was risking a lot for me and I would never let her down.

Over the next couple of months, we started making plans for her to move. Every time I went to Dallas, I would bring back a load of her stuff and store it in the spare bedroom.

During the week, she was working to deal with her house and things that she could not or did not want to bring with her. Items like furniture, chickens, and horses. She had to plan for all of this, and she worked hard to get it done.

I also prepared for her arrival, I stored her stuff in an extra room until she would get settled in and could add her touch to the house. I reorganized my closet and took up my two cubic feet and left her the other two hundred feet.

Even though the day was coming when she would move, we still did not want to be apart on the weekends, so I continued to drive to Dallas every weekend until the day we moved her in for good.

I know it must have been a little scary for her to be moving away. I mean, she had lived close to that area her entire life and moving away after all those years could not be easy, but she never let it show.

I left work early on a Friday and drove to Dallas and spent the weekend with her and when I left that Sunday morning, she was following me. We had both vehicles loaded down with the rest of her things and it was a long drive.

When we arrived, we took some time to enjoy the moment. We went twenty-three years without seeing or hearing from each other, and somehow here we are.

As we unpacked the vehicles and got settled in together, I thought about how many things had to click into place for this to happen. What are the odds that this would come together this way? After a few minutes, I decided not to think about it and just be grateful.

We managed to get everything unloaded and put out of the way before the fatigue caused by travelling and moving caught up with us. We slept hard on our first night of living together in twenty-three years.

Chapter 12 - Adjustments

I went back to work on the Monday morning after we moved Kristy into our home. I should say new home because everything changed for both of us, but I did not have to make as many adjustments as she did.

One adjustment she had to make was being farther away from her family. I know this was a hard one for her and it still is to this day. I try to make it easier and I am working on a long-term goal of getting her closer to them but for now, she continues to tough it out.

Another thing she had to adjust to, and this is a big one was my son. They did not hit it off in the beginning and I know that was painful for her. She wanted to be a great stepmom, but he did not make it easy on her. He is very stubborn, like his dad and a teenager and this is a bad combination when someone is actively trying to care about you.

In the past, when I tried to have a relationship, my son was able to drive a wedge and protect his territory and to him, this was no different. Even though I explained that it was different, he still tried. I do not believe that he realized what he was doing but that is beside the point.

He had no idea that this woman was my soul mate, and nothing could drive us apart ever again. How could he know?

There were some hard times that the two of them went through and it was painful for me as well. I mean, these were two of the most important people in the world to me and I wanted them to get along.

I will not go into too much detail because this book is about love and negativity has no place here. Just know that in the end, everything straightened out and we are a family now and that is what is important.

Another adjustment she had to make was being with a man that is highly driven and wants to be the best he can be. That sounds like a good thing until you are the one that must put up with me.

Living with me can be tough. I work too much, and I enjoy working so that means I do not generally want a vacation from my work. I also take risks that most people would not dare, and this stress can be transferred from me to her.

I also do not ease up on myself on the weekends so sleeping in or taking it easy never happen with me. If she asked me to stop, I would but she rarely does this because she wants me to be happy too.

Occasionally, I make myself take a break and go out with her just for fun. Do not get me wrong, making her happy is my top priority. I always try to do things that make her happy. I am extremely focused on my career, but I am committed to her and her happiness. When she moved here, we made a promise to each other to never spend the night apart and we have never broken that promise.

I also had to make a few adjustments, but I always embrace change, I am kind of weird like that. I had been single for a long time and I was used to leaving something in the morning and it being the same when I got home and that was an adjustment for me. It took me a while to adjust to having someone else in my space, but I was happy to make the adjustment.

I also had to adjust to the feeling of having someone to come home to. Having someone that cared about me and wanted to be around for everything was a huge change for me. It was a great change and it made my entire world better knowing that Kristy was there with me along the way.

Chapter 13 – A Happy New Year

We had been living together for a while, but I am not sure if it had been a year yet when I decided to take the next step. I shopped for a while and finally bought a wedding ring. It was white gold with a cluster of small diamonds. I had a fairly good idea of what she would like because I had been paying attention to her reactions for a while. I thought it was the perfect ring and I hoped she would too.

I carried the ring around in my pocket for a week or so waiting for the right time to ask her to marry me. I must have seemed weird a few times during this week when I would work up to it and then change suddenly because the moment was not right, but I did not care.

I would get close to doing it and then I would lose my nerve, or the conversation would change gears, or the timing would be inappropriate so I would back out. Several times, she asked me if everything was ok so I must have looked like a goof.

I had brokered huge business deals with people that were much more advanced than me and never been this nervous. I had been an ironworker hanging from a small piece of steel a couple of hundred feet in the air before and not been nervous so why now?

We were getting ready to go out for dinner one evening and the moment aligned, and it was the perfect time. I had considered doing it in public, but I was afraid I would embarrass her and besides, she is not big on making a scene. This moment turned out to be perfect because it caught her by surprise and the conversation seemed to be right.

This moment was not meant for the public, it was meant for the two of us. It was a moment that we shared that forever changed us. I often think back to that moment and it always makes me smile.

I sometimes think about the moment when she said yes and remember her smile and her tears, and I wonder if I am everything, she hoped I would be.

We thought about it for a while and decided to get married on new years eve. The timing was right for us and it felt right. New year new life.

We had a small but beautiful wedding and it was one of the happiest days of my life. Not only did I get married to a beautiful woman, but I also married my soul mate and my best friend.

We postponed our honeymoon because we had a tight schedule at the time but when we do finally go on our honeymoon, we are going to do it right. I know, I should have arranged this and gotten it done before now but we have been working on big dreams and we both feel the same about it.

Chapter 14 – Happiness

We are a happily married couple and we would not dream of spending a night apart, but we also recognize that we are two people and we each have lives.

Although she has made me the happiest man in the world and does so every day, it is not her responsibility to make me happy. It is also not my responsibility to make her happy even though I try my best every day to keep her smiling and laughing.

I believe that in life we are all responsible for our own happiness. If you cannot make yourself happy, no one else will be able to make you happy either, at least not for long.

Kristy and I are two independently happy people that have decided to spend the rest of our live together. We are soul mates and we make each other's lives better and I cannot imagine it any other way.

There are times when we help each other through a tough or sad moment, and we are always happy to do this for each other, but I say again, our core happiness comes from within ourselves. We choose to share that happiness with each other.

When it comes to happiness, finding a balance can be tricky but for me it seems effortless. Working towards my goals and making Kristy smile are some of the things that make me happy.

I also love seeing our kids and grandkids smile and learn and enjoy life. When the kids and grandbabies are happy, I know my wife is happy. Nothing puts a smile on her face like seeing them happy.

Chapter 15 - From There to Here

I want to back up for a minute and talk about where we started from and where we are now. I will not dig too deep, but I want to lay it all out in a short summary so we can see the starting point and the current point.

Twenty-five years ago, I met Kristy and she was young and beautiful. I knew I would love her if I got to know her.

What she met was a young kid that had pretty much nothing to his name except a truck, some clothes and a work ethic that was better than most.

When I say work ethic, I mean in the sense that I worked hard while I was at work. I allowed no one to out work me. That did not always extend to showing up on time.

I was young and had no idea of what I was doing but I worked hard, came home to her, and we tried to enjoy our lives and it seemed to fall into place.

After some time, I managed to screw up everything and my mistakes had a ripple effect that caused us to walk away from each other for what we thought was forever. We thought we would just forget about each other and go on with our lives and we did just that, almost.

We walked away from each other and got on with our lives, but we did not forget about each other. In fact, we remember more about the time we spent together back then than we do about many more recent parts of our lives.

We began thinking about each other twenty-three years later and ended up reconnecting, falling in love all over again and getting married. We have grown as a couple, as individuals and we are all around better people than we were when we were apart.

We are now past the honeymoon stage where we spend every possible moment together, but we still would never dream of spending a night apart. I am an early riser and she is a late-night person, so we do have some time where we function without each other, but we are happy with that.

I get my early mornings to myself and she gets the whole house to herself at night. It works out exactly right for us. I think it is important to find that balance where you get enough time with each other, but you still get some time alone.

We never pass by each other without a kiss and saying I love you and we do things for each other regularly. It is nice to have this connection between us and I know that it would be hard to live without it.

Chapter 16 - Drastic Changes

This section may or may not belong in a book about love and soul mates, but I feel it is relevant.

When we were together all those years ago, I was working as an Iron Worker and I acted the part. I was tough, showed little emotion and expected the same from others. I was also young and easily influenced so I found myself changing often.

If someone had a convincing argument on a topic, I would often believe them and jump on that bandwagon and spread information that I did not necessarily know to be true. In short, I was a young guy that was finding my way.

When Kristy met me for the first time as adults, I was a different person but still had and have the same playful heart. I put little value into appearing tough and a lot of value into helping others and growing myself. I had a corporate office and my mindset was focused on leadership and management.

This time around, I was a grown man and I had already found my way. There was little doubt inside of me and my confidence level was high.

This information is relevant because all those years ago, I was exactly what she needed me to be. She kept a picture of me in her head from back then and it matched her level at the time.

I did the same with her. She was exactly what I needed back then, and she is exactly what I need in my life right now but neither of us are the same person we were back then. We have grown into different people than we were back then, and this allows us to still be a perfect match.

If I had been the Steve, she dated so many years ago, she would not be able to stand me today because she has grown into the person she is now. While I see her memory as a great one and my heart still loves any version of her, she is a different person than she was then. If she were the same, she may not think much of the Steve that I am today.

While we were apart, we both followed our own paths and we still do that today. I have a routine that is mine and she has her own routine and we invite each other into those routines all the time.

It is amazing how much we think alike and how similar our senses of humor are. We are truly soul mates and I have no idea how I made it for so long without having her in my life.

Chapter 17 - Family Rollercoaster

Between our two families, we are always missing someone and wanting to go visit someone.

Being an entrepreneur make it difficult to take off and visit family so we must be strategic about when we take our trips, but I can tell when it is time to bring Momma to visit her kids.

I never hesitate when it is time because she took a big chance on me by moving here and leaving the area that she grew up in and lived her entire life. I also observe the fact that if you stand between a mother and her kids, she may just destroy you! That is a joke, I miss the kids and grand kids the same as she does, and I love all our visits and trips that we get to spend together.

Like any other family, we have many different personalities involved in ours. You name it, we have it in our family. This makes our visits interesting and offers a variety of conversation.

As for me, I am one of the types that loves to joke and play when I can. When I am working, I try to stay focused but when I am not, I will joke about almost anything.

When I was younger, I thought that I was missing the ability to take things seriously. During serious situations, I was always trying to lighten the situation and I had a special ability to make a joke too soon.

I was told that I need to consider other people's feelings and that my jokes were insensitive, and I needed to feel empathy, but the truth is, no one saw things the way I saw them. I was never trying to be harsh or hurt anyone, I was trying to help them get through the tough times.

My sense of humor has been one of my greatest assets to me and I wanted to share it with others. I still do this, but I am a little better with timing than I once was.

Anytime something tries to get me down, I can almost always depend on my sense of humor to pull me away from the darkness and get me back on my feet so when I see others in pain, it is a reflex to try to make them laugh. Sometimes this still backfires but it is always worth a shot.

My wife has a similar personality to mine which keeps her from killing me. She is funny and quick witted but not quite as confident as I am. She will often hold back her sense of humor until she is provoked but once you open that door, watch out.

We often make fun of each other, as we always have, and I cannot remember one time when our playfulness was taken out of context. Laughing at ourselves is one of our greatest assets.

When we make fun of each other and laugh at ourselves, it allows us to point out funny things about each other without either of us feeling like our relationship is in danger. This makes it a good form of communication as well as a good time.

Of course, if there is a real problem, we sit down and talk it out like adults. When I know that I have been focused on work for too long, I immediately apologize to her and ask her what she wants to do. I also explain why I was so absorbed by work and assure her that she is more important than work. She does the same for me.

Chapter 18 – Finding our groove

Kristy and I have gone through many different stages of our relationship since we reconnected.

We went through the stage where we were together all the time for months. I mean we never spent a moment apart that was not necessary. It was a great feeling to be that close to someone.

It seemed like that feeling could not be topped and then it seemed like more things came along that made it necessary to spend a little time apart.

We started businesses and that required us to spend time apart. As we spent a little time apart, I noticed another great feeling that started to form. The feeling of being apart and still feeling like your other half is with you. It is amazing to be loved so much that it feels like you are together, even when you are not.

Right now, we are in the stage where we spend time together, work together and we take a few hours each evening to have time to ourselves. I do my thing and she does her thing and we are both happy.

My afternoons are spent unwinding. I am either reading, writing, or watching television. It is my way of disconnecting from the world of business.

When I do watch television, I watch senseless shows. The last thing I want to watch is reality TV. Afterall, I am trying to get away from the real world for a while.

Kristy likes to sit on the porch and talk on the phone to her mother and Nanny for hours at a time. I get to join in on the conversation occasionally and they are a lot of fun to talk to. I can see why she enjoys it so much.

Another thing that causes us to spend more time apart is that my days are utilized mostly in the mornings. I enjoy being awake and active at four in the morning, my wife, not so much.

I wake up and cannot wait to start my day. I am tired and sleepy just like anyone else but my desire to own the day and the level of control that I have developed do not let that slow me down.

If my wife does not have a need to get up early, she would rather sleep in and that is how she enjoys her morning. There is no right or wrong way in my mind, but this time offset does reduce that amount of time we spend together.

When we do visit each other's time zones, it is like getting a treat. We get to enjoy a little of each other's time that we do not normally get. This ties back to each of us having our own lives and inviting the other into them.

Chapter 19 - What is Next?

As we catch up to where we are today, I want to start closing out this book and talking about what is next. I know there is value in being spontaneous and plans tend to change but I believe we must have some sort of plan if we are going to sit in the driver's seat.

The plan that we have laid out for ourselves is simple. Of course, our plans change as we grow but these high-level plans are stable even the details change often.

For our careers, we want to make our businesses successful and leave a legacy for our children and grandchildren. We also want to help others reach their goals along the way.

If we reach our goals and never help anyone else reach theirs, it will be an empty victory. Reaching a life goal is worth all the effort you put into it, but it is not fulfilling unless you take the time to help other people.

By helping other people, you get the greatest gift. You get to know what it is like to give something away. I am not talking helping someone that can help you reach your goal; I am talking about helping someone that has no way of ever repaying you. When you do that, you will know what I mean.

As for our lives, we want to have a nice place to live that the children and grandchildren want to visit and be able to spend lots of time with them. At the same time, we must have chickens because the wife loves taking care of them. We also must have water of some kind. The water condition is for me. I love the water. I would prefer a beach or a lake, but I will settle for a pool if it comes to that.

I would not pass up the perfect home just because it is not on a lake, but you can be certain that I will be looking for the perfect place that is on the lake first.

Another thing that is next is getting our families together more often. We spend so much time focused on business that we find it hard to make time to see our families. This is unacceptable but we have chosen to make do for a short time so we can get our lives in order.

I asked Kristy what is next, and her first answer was, "why are you asking me that wierdo?" but then she thought about it for a while and she wants us to drive our businesses forward and be the best we can be at them. That is a pretty amazing response, if you ask me but that is what I expect from her.

For me, I intend to build the largest and best companies that I possibly can and at the same time force my family to buy or build bookshelves because I have so many books and they feel obligated to buy them. That is a joke, but I do intend to write many books. In fact, I want to write books all the time, no matter what else is going on in my life.

I intend to write books forever until I either have nothing more to write about or until I die. If I am living and in my right mind, I will continue to grow so I should always have something to write about. I may even try to write a fiction book one of these days but that will be a huge shift for me.

Ending this book is bittersweet for me. It is exciting to get this finished and work on publishing it and at the same time, there is so much more that can be said and talked about.

I have tried to simplify feelings and situations in this book and not get caught up in my own feelings and this may make it seem less complicated. I do not want to falsely represent what a typical relationship is because there is no typical when it comes to love.

Many of the scenarios in this book involved emotions that it would be difficult to express in words. There are times when we have been angry at each other and times when we felt our hearts could not hold the amount of love we feel for each other and through it all, we remain strong because we know we are together forever.

I hope you have enjoyed this short book about the love that did not die, even after twenty years of being dormant.

Thanks for reading,

SKB

www.ingramcontent.com/pod-product-compliance
Lightning Source LLC
Chambersburg PA
CBHW031310060426
42444CB00033B/1168